AMERICA AT THE CROSSROADS

Great Photographs from the Thirties

H-18

AMERICA AT THE CROSSROADS

Great Photographs from the Thirties

Edited by
Jerome Prescott

SMITHMARK

This edition published in 1995 by SMITHMARK Publishers Inc., 16 East 32nd Street, New York, New York 10016.

SMITHMARK books are available for bulk purchase for sales promotion and premium use. For details write or telephone the Manager of Special Sales, SMITHMARK Publishers Inc., 16 East 32nd Street, New York, NY 10016. (212) 532-6600.

Produced by Brompton Books Corp., 15 Sherwood Place, Greenwich, CT 06830.

ISBN 0-8317-0739-9

Printed in China

10 9 8 7 6 5 4 3 2 1

Photo credits:
All of the photographs in this book were obtained from the Library of Congress, with the following exceptions:
Caldwell Berkovic Gallery: pages 52, 53
National Archives: pages 1, 2, 7, 10, 12, 19, 23, 26, 27, 28, 34, 35, 40, 41, 42, 43, 44, 45, 49, 50, 51, 54, 55, 56, 88, 89, 96 (both), 97, 98, 99, 103, 104, 105
Norton Collection, from Colorado social services: pages 46 (both), 47 (both), 101 (both)
Public Library Archives, San Francisco: pages 36 (both), 37, 64, 65, 81, 95
US Department of the Interior: pages 5, 20, 21, 22, 24, 25, 29, 30, 31, 32, 33, 39, 63, 90, 91, 102, 115

Page 1:

Lewis Hine
Local Man
(Tennessee, 1933)

Even before the creation of the Resettlement Administration and the Farm Security Administration and their photographic section, the Tennessee Valley Authority (TVA) employed photographers such as Lewis Hine to document the regions of rural Tennessee, Kentucky, Alabama and Mississippi that the TVA's activities would impact.

Page 2:

Lewis Hine
Wash Day
(Tennessee, 1933)

Life in the regions of the South that Hine documented for the TVA seemed unbelievably primitive as viewed through the eyes of someone accustomed to life in the urban eastern cities.

Facing page:

George Alexander Grant
Grenier's Store
(Devil's Tower National Monument, Wyoming, 1933)

En route to a photo shoot at Devil's Tower National Monument in Wyoming on 7 June 1933, Grant stopped near the Belle Fourche River Bridge to document Grenier's Store, possibly to purchase a soft drink, and to chat with these three forlorn children. Like many such establishments on the lonely, often unpaved byways of the nation, Grenier's also sold gasoline and served as the local post office. A lunch counter was next door and a cabin camp across the road offered accomodations to those few travellers who passed this way during the Depression. Roadside businesses such as this one struggled during the 1930s, but thrived after World War II—if they survived.

INTRODUCTION

America was at a crossroads in the 1930s. It was a turning point sandwiched between two World Wars, between the industrial revolution of the nineteenth century and the technological revolution of the latter half of the twentieth century. America was at a point where there would be deep political and economic changes, but it was as much, if not more so, a cultural and social crossroads. It was a crossroads for which the catalyst, the traffic signal if you will, was an economic disaster that was largely unexpected, a disaster whose duration was entirely unexpected.

It began with the legendary 'Crash' of the New York Stock Exchange on 29 October 1929, the day that was remembered with horror by an entire generation as 'Black Tuesday.' It was an economic disaster of unparalleled proportions that engulfed an entire generation, the entire industrialized world, and it lasted for more than a decade. It was the Great Depression.

The causes of the disaster have been considered and debated by economists and social historians for more than half a century. The fact was that after a decade of enormous growth, the world economy virtually collapsed. Consumer spending and business investment faltered. By 1931, business investment in the United States had fallen to less than five percent of its 1929 levels. By 1932, it was virtually nonexistent.

At first people tried to pretend that it hadn't happened. Motor car king Henry Ford raised wages. President Herbert Hoover lowered taxes and shrugged that it was just a minor twitch in the economy. Recalling the previous economic calamities of 1873 and 1893, which were known in the vernacular as 'Panics,' he coined the phrase 'Depression' to make people feel better. In fact, Hoover's 'Depression' lasted longer and sank deeper than even the Panic of 1893.

As consumer spending fell, businesses sold fewer products and thus needed fewer workers. When businesses cut their work force, they created a vast population of unemployed people who could barely afford to eat, much less buy consumer goods.

From a more than comfortable lifestyle amid a fabulously expansive economy in the 'Roaring Twenties,' the American people tumbled into the abyss of the Great Depression.

America was at the crossroads. The nation that had tamed the

Facing page:

Lewis Hine
Plowing on the Mountainside
(Tennessee, 1933)

Awareness of, and sympathy with, the plight of the farmers, including southern tenant farmers and hill people, was very much a fact in literary circles in the 1930s.

Erskine Caldwell's *Tobacco Road* (1932) and *God's Little Acre* (1933) were immensely popular and led to a proletarian school of literature. This, in turn, led to a great deal of interest in the kind of photographs that Hine was taking.

vast frontier only a generation before found itself facing a new kind of turning point—a decisive moment that came with maturity. There was no longer a vast horizon. The geographical limitations of the nation had been reached. Like the tiny nations of Europe whom she had superseded as the world's preeminent economy, America was coming to grips with the reality of being finite.

America at the crossroads was a different nation than the America of the frontiersmen. America at the crossroads was a different nation than the America of the fresh-faced doughboys who'd gone off to Europe in 1917 to save exhausted Europeans from themselves.

Many historians blame Hoover for the Great Depression, but the causes were complex and generally beyond his control. His real sin was to minimize its seriousness and to allow himself to be seen as having squandered three years doing little to help the increasing number of people who were suffering because of it.

In 1932, Hoover ran for re-election against New York Governor Franklin Delano Roosevelt, an activist candidate who promised massive government intervention to relieve the people from the horrors of the Depression. That was the message that the people wanted to hear and Roosevelt buried Hoover in a landslide.

The voters gave him a mandate and he gave them what they wanted. An inspirational father figure, Roosevelt also delivered on his promises, at least so far as the scale of his intervention in the economy. His agenda, which he described as the New Deal, included a vast archipelago of public works projects—from the Works Progress Administration (WPA) to the Civilian Conservation Corps (CCC)—aimed at putting the unemployed to work building roads, government buildings and other projects.

The New Deal also is remembered for the Roosevelt Administration's keen interest in the arts. Among the first elements of this interest were the Public Works Art Project of 1933, and the Section of Painting & Sculpture created at the Treasury Department by Edward Bruce in 1934.

The latter, in turn, led to the Treasury Relief Art Program under the WPA and eventually to a broad-ranging Federal Art Project (FAP), guided by such visionary administrators as Jacob Baker, who appointed scholar and art historian Holger Cahill to head the program.

The Federal Art Project provided incredible examples of public representational art that reached its apogee in the great murals in the federal buildings of the 1930s. The Federal Writers' Project (FWP) put as many as 6000 unemployed

writers to work producing travel guides to America, collecting oral histories and folklore, and producing a great verbal portrait of America at the crossroads.

It is interesting to look back on how government-sponsored art flourished in almost an academically classical form during the 1930s, after the 1920s had witnessed the formative years of such uniquely American forms of art as skyscrapers, Hollywood cinema and jazz.

A corollary of this was that the American people were exposed to a greater range of works of grand public visual art on a classical scale (albeit of contemporary *style*) than at any time previously.

No portraits of America at the crossroads can compare, however, to the brilliant photography of the period. The photographers documented this momentous time in moving portraits and lucid landscapes that still touch us deeply and help to define our image of ourselves as Americans.

The photographers themselves were generally young, well educated, energetic and visionary. They included a virtual who's who of the founders of modern documentary photography: Dorothea Lange, Walker Evans, Carl Mydans, Arthur Rothstein, John Vachon, Marion Post Wolcott, Ben Shahn; their names were like milestones in a time when photography was coming into its own as a medium of social commentary.

At the same time, people such as George Alexander Grant were at work, documenting other facets of the American crossroads for other agencies, such as, in Grant's case, the Department of the Interior. Grant also documented the activities of the New Deal agencies as they came into contact with places administered by the Department of the Interior. For example, among the Grant photos included in this portfolio, is one taken at Canyon de Chelly National Monument on 21 September 1934 as a group of Navajo gathered for a presentation from personnel of the Soil Conservation Service.

The centerpiece of any portfolio of photographs from this era—especially federal documentary photography—must certainly be the work produced by the photographic section of the Resettlement Administration (RA), which later became the Farm Security Administration (FSA).

Farmers, especially those in mid-America, had been particularly hard hit by the Depression. Not only had the Depression taken its toll on consumption of farm products, but an unusually severe drought had turn several midwestern states—notably Oklahoma—into what was known as the 'Dust Bowl.'

One of the now-forgotten facts of rural life in the 1930s was

Facing page:

Arthur Rothstein
Farmer and Sons Walking in the Face of a Dust Storm
(Cimarron County, Oklahoma, 1936)

Arthur Rothstein's photograph of the farmer and his sons struggling through the blizzard of dust has become an icon of the Dust Bowl era.

The Depression took its toll on the farmers, but when an unusually severe drought had turned several midwestern states—notably Oklahoma—into what was a literal Dust Bowl, it wrought havoc on families who had made a living from this land for generations.

that in much of the South and Mountain West, electricity was simply unavailable to those living outside towns or cities. To address this shortcoming, as well as to create jobs, the New Deal embarked on great electrification projects. These ranged from huge hydroelectric projects in the Tennessee Valley and the Pacific Northwest to stringing hundreds of miles of power lines. This led to the creation of such agencies as the Tennessee Valley Authority (TVA) and the Rural Electrification Administration (REA).

Just as the FSA was organized to serve the needs of farmers while employing photographers, both the TVA and REA provided aid to farmers (in the form of inexpensive electricity) and employed photographers to document their activities.

Awareness of, and sympathy with, the plight of the farmers, particularly Dust Bowl refugees and the unlanded southern tenant farmers known as 'sharecroppers,' was very much a fact in literary circles in the 1930s. Erskine Caldwell's *Tobacco Road* (1932) and *God's Little Acre* (1933) were immensely popular and led to a proletarian school of literature that was best characterized by John Steinbeck's *Grapes of Wrath* (1939), which dealt with the flight of Oklahoma's rural poor—the 'Okies'—to California.

In fact, much of the work of the FSA photographers included subjects that went beyond the farm to life in the cities, small towns and in the migrant worker and Dust Bowl refugee camps which were surrogate towns for a generation of displaced Americans.

Headed by Roy Stryker, the photographic section of the FSA was born in 1935 as the photographic section of the Resettlement Administration (RA), which itself evolved into the FSA in 1937. The section remained with the FSA until 1942, when it was transferred to the Domestic Operations Branch of the Office of War Information (OWI).

The Resettlement Administration, like the FSA, was conceived as an agency to help displaced farmers and victims of the Dust Bowl. The photographic section had the task of documenting and publicizing the agency's activities. They were released to the news media and many were widely published during the 1930s and early 1940s.

On one level it can be said that Stryker and his photographers gave us one of the most accurate and certainly the most longlasting views of life during the Great Depression.

In the beginning, Stryker gave a great deal of latitude to his photographers, trusting their documentary sense and allowing their perceptions to guide their work. This was in contrast to the

activities of the then-popular pictorial magazines, such as *Collier's*, *Life* and *Look*, who covered the same themes, but whose photographers were given specific assignments, and whose articles spoke to specific, preconceived themes. On the other hand, the magazines also published photographs released by the FSA. It is interesting to note, however, that some of the FSA photographers, such as Carl Mydans, went on to distinguished careers with the major magazines during and after World War II.

Indeed, most of the important photographers of the era were trained in New York and, as such, they had both the technical skills and the well-rounded aesthetic sensibilities that were necessary to create images that were truly art and not simply snapshots.

Walker Evans came to the Resettlement Administration in 1935, already one of America's best-known documentary photographers. The fact that a man of his stature wound up working for a government agency is indicative of how bad things had gotten for artists in the 1930s. Even after he returned to New York City in 1938, he continued to accept assignments from Stryker.

Jack Delano studied at the Pennsylvania Academy of Fine Arts and came to the FSA in 1940 when he was 26. Roy Stryker sent him on numerous assignments, including Puerto Rico, where he documented the economic development work being

undertaken under the direction of Rexford Tugwell, an old friend of Stryker's and one of the men who influenced the decision to set up a photographic section within the Resettlement Administration.

Dorothea Lange is today recognized as one of the greatest documentary photographers of the twentieth century. Born Dorothea Nutzhorn in Hoboken, New Jersey, she grew up in New York City and apprenticed in the studio of Arnold Genthe, one of the great figures in the early days of documentary photography. She moved to San Francisco in 1918 at the age of 24 and took her mother's maiden name as her surname.

In San Francisco, Lange worked as a commercial portrait photographer, but with the onset of the Depression, both she and her husband, painter Maynard Dixon, fell on hard times. She eventually began a socially conscious documentation of the hard times that were engulfing the people, often working with Professor Paul Taylor, who was studying the Depression for the University of California, and who she married after her divorce from Dixon in 1935.

In 1934, both Taylor and Lange worked for California's State Emergency Relief Administration, but as Roy Stryker became aware of Lange's work, he offered her a job with the RA in 1935. Her documentation of life in the migrant worker camps of California's Central Valley have become icons of Depression-era photography.

There were, in fact, some truly important images recorded during this era by photographers working for state agencies. Edward Wall Norton's work with Colorado's state relief agency is probably among the best. He specialized in cross-generational studies, and his photographs, particularly his images of grandparents with very young children, attracted a good deal of attention, especially when they were exhibited in the late 1940s.

Edward Mancuso was one of Dorothea Lange's contemporaries in San Francisco. While she worked as a commercial portrait photographer before the Depression, Mancuso cut his teeth as a news photographer with one of the city's now long defunct daily papers. He is best remembered for his moving images of the terrible labor unrest that culminated in the notorious General Strike that paralyzed San Francisco in July 1934.

Unlike the REA, TVA and FSA photographers who were in government service for only a few years, George Alexander Grant worked for the Interior Department's US National Park Service from the 1920s until well after World War II. While Grant's most famous works were his great landscapes of the

Left:

Lewis Hine
Mountain Woman
(Tennessee, 1933)

The remarkable studies that Hine created during his work with the TVA included images that were almost stereotypically ideal, and which fostered an entire genre of treasured icons.

national parks, he took many photographs during the 1930s and early 1940s that help round out our picture of America at the crossroads.

An Illinois native, Russell Lee had an instinctive, albeit often unrealistic, interest in farming and farm life. Like the urban elite of the 1960s who imagined a rural utopia 'on the land,' he idealized farm life and the joys of small town America as an almost ethereal place. Fortunately, his FSA photography captures main street America at that point where main street intersects the crossroads.

Marion Post Wolcott was a New Jersey-born professional photographer who had travelled in Europe for several years before joining the FSA in 1938. At the age of 28, she was older than many of the other FSA photographers, although much younger than Dorothea Lange. She had also evolved a distinctive personal style. Stryker criticized her for her long hair and brightly colored scarves and flowered dresses, which he felt would detract from her ability to move among the people whom she would photograph. By this time, he had come to accept the biased view that the reality of America was more in the faces of Lange's migrant workers than in the faces of the folks on Main Street. Marion Post taught him that the reality of the 1930s had many sides. Remembered for her vision and sensitivity, she stunned her colleagues by giving up documentary photography after her marriage to Lee Wolcott in 1941.

Arthur Rothstein was a college student from New York City when he got his first assignment from Stryker in 1935. As an FSA photographer, he travelled far and wide, from the cotton fields of Alabama to the cattle ranches of Montana.

Ben Shahn was a Lithuanian-born commercial photographer who grew up in New York City, where he worked as a commercial photographer. He and Walker Evans were roommates for a time and were both very much a part of the arts scene in New York. After his years with the FSA, Shahn put his camera aside to take up a successful career as a painter.

John Vachon, born and raised in Minnesota, had come to Washington, DC to attend college and started with the FSA as an errand-boy. With a bit of technical advice from the New York-trained Shahn and Evans, he took up a camera in 1937 and went on the road in 1938. His photographs, which are literally snapshots, are a cross-section of American life at the crossroads of the nation's epic history.

Another aspect of American life at the crossroads in the 1930s was the enormous construction projects that were undertaken. Out of scale with most previous projects, they were made possible by the availability of inexpensive skilled labor. New York's towering skyscrapers and San Francisco's huge bridges were among these projects. The Empire State Building was completed in 1931 and the Golden Gate Bridge was opened in 1937.

These magnificent efforts were recorded on film by numerous photographers, but among the most memorable images are Lewis Hine's views of the fast-growing Manhattan skyline and Benjamin W Smith's views of the construction of the Golden Gate Bridge. Hine later went into the Tennessee Valley to record the people that would be served by the TVA electrification projects.

Born in Canada and raised in New York City, Smith came west to San Francisco to work as an engineer on the bridge project. His photographs, taken mainly in 1936, are among the most exquisite that exist, and amazingly, they came to light only following his death in 1992.

Meanwhile, the Harmon Foundation and the Commission on the Church and Race Relations of the Federal Council of Churches sponsored a number of exhibitions of African-American art. Their goal was to acquaint the public with the artistic and creative abilities of African-Americans. Kenneth F Space, a photographer with the Harmon Foundation, travelled through the South in 1936 and 1937, photographing life in the black community. Many of his photographs were taken of artists at work or students on college campuses. His work provides a stark contrast to Arthur Rothstein's photographs of rural African-Americans.

While George Alexander Grant's work enjoyed a good deal of regional popularity, particularly in the Southwest, much of the FSA work was largely unseen during the two decades following World War II. These images were to be 'rediscovered' by succeeding generations of socially conscious curators and viewers in the late 1960s and again in the early 1990s. For example, Dorothea Lange's work was the subject of a major show at the Museum of Modern Art in New York in 1966 (a year after her death) and at the Museum of Modern Art in San Francisco in 1994. By this time the images were no longer current news, but a poignant form of historical documentation recognized as a high form of art.

These works are important because they were created under unique circumstances by photographers who were also great artists, photographers who were allowed to express their own creativity in a way that is seldom possible for commercial photographers.

The years of the Depression were a distinct, albeit distant, moment. The nation was at a crossroads. Torn by the Great Depression, the land and its people stood with one foot in the rural traditions of an earlier century and the other on the threshold of the promise of a better, bolder future that, for most people, was near enough to imagine, but just too distant to touch.

Dorothea Lange. Walker Evans. George Alexander Grant. Carl Mydans. Arthur Rothstein. John Vachon. Marion Post Wolcott. Ben Shahn. These are the portraits of a people and their time, when adversity molded character like a sculptor carves stone, as captured on film by a new generation of photographers who were at the dawn of greatness.

PLATE 1

Ben Shahn
Cotton Pickers on the
Alexander Plantation
(Pulaski County, Arkansas, 1935)

It was during the autumn of 1935 that Ben Shahn made his first trip into the South on assignment with the Resettlement Administration (RA). Although another agency paid for his travel expenses, the RA paid for his film. These photographs of cotton pickers were taken on the Alexander Plantation in Pulaski County, Arkansas.

PLATE 2

Ben Shahn
Cotton Pickers
(Pulaski County, Arkansas, 1935)

Shahn took these photographs of cotton pickers on the Alexander Plantation in Pulaski County at 6:30 on a cool fall morning.

PLATE 3

Dorothea Lange
*Migrant Mother, Florence Thompson,
and Her Children*
(Nipomo, California, 1936)

During 1934 and 1935, Lange's work
with California's State Emergency Relief
Administration had given her an over-
view of sites worthy of documentary
photography. In March 1936, she went
out to the migrant camp near Nipomo in
the coastal valley of southern San Luis
Obispo County, where she took a series
of photographs of Florence Thompson
and her children.

PLATE 4

Dorothea Lange
*Migrant Mother, Florence Thompson,
and Her Children*
(Nipomo, California, 1936)

Lange's documentation of the migrant
worker camps of California's agricultural
regions has resulted in some of the best
known icons of Depression-era photography. Lange's classic portrait of Florence
Thompson is now a prized museum
piece, with prints worth up to $30,000.
Museum curators have, however, given
little thought to what became of Ms
Thompson herself.

PLATE 5

Dorothea Lange
Alone on a California Highway
(Central Valley, California, 1935)

During 1934, Dorothea Lange had worked for California's State Emergency Relief Administration, but as Roy Stryker became aware of Lange's work, he offered her a job with the Resettlement Administration (RA) in 1935. Her documentation of life in the migrant worker camps of California's Central Valley was destined to provide us with many important icons of Depression-era photography.

PLATE 6

Dorothea Lange
Farmer With Sheep
(Hayward, California, 1936)

While Lange's documentation of the migrant workers is well known, it is important to note that she also documented farmers who were still in business and workers who had found jobs. The Farm Security Administration needed success stories just as it needed to show human misery.

PLATE 7

George Alexander Grant
Linda Hall at Mesa Verde
(Mesa Verde National Monument,
Colorado, 1929)

The calm before the crossroads: During
the last summer of the 1920s, when the
Crash and the Depression were still un-
imaginable, George Alexander Grant
travelled the Southwest, visiting the national parks and using them to frame an
occasional artistic, less documentary, in-
terpretation. Ms Hall was a young tour-
ist from East Liverpool, Ohio.

PLATE 8

George Alexander Grant
Emmett Harryson at Mesa Verde
(Mesa Verde National Monument,
Colorado, 1929)

Mesa Verde had seen Depressions on a
smaller, yet disastrous, scale. Centuries
before Emmett Harryson posed for
Grant, the civilization of the prehistoric
native peoples who built Mesa Verde had
come to an end in a cycle of drought
which, by comparison, made the Dust
Bowl seem insignificant.

PLATE 9

George Alexander Grant
*National Park Service Ranger atop
the Ruins at Mesa Verde*
(Mesa Verde National Monument,
Colorado, 1929)

Grant visited Mesa Verde National Monument on 10 August 1929, a still, hot day in the summer before Black Tuesday. Wall Street seemed light years away, but soon its ripples would be felt, even here. America was at the crossroads, though few could see the change coming, especially in the timeless serenity of the Southwest. Ranger Beutel was from New Orleans.

PLATE 10

Lewis Hine
Workmen Bolting Together the Framework of the Empire State Building
(New York City, New York, 1930)

In contrast with Grant's views of the rugged West and FSA views of rural farm country, was another aspect of American life at the crossroads of the 1930s.

The enormous construction projects that were undertaken included many of New York's towering skyscrapers, and among the most important images are Lewis Hine's photographs of the Empire State Building. America's tallest building for over four decades, the 102-story building was built in only one year, being completed in May 1931.

Plates 11 & 12

George Alexander Grant
*A Promotional Film Crew Camping
at Piegan Pass*
(Glacier National Park,
Montana, 1932)

George Alexander Grant's work for the National Park Service changed little as the nation fell into what was perhaps the worst year of the Depression. Although he primarily photographed the scenic beauty of the national parks, he spent a portion of this excursion into Glacier's back country documenting a film crew. Their assignment was to film a documentary of the national parks.

PLATE 13

Lewis Hine
One Room Schoolhouse
(Tennessee, 1933)

When he arrived in the hill country of Tennessee and Kentucky, Hine discovered a lifestyle that was, in many respects, unchanged since the first half of the nineteenth century.

While today we may look on a one room school with nostalgic fondness, it was viewed by urban easterners in 1933 as a symptom of a backwardness that required remedial action.

PLATE 14

Lewis Hine
Straining Jelly
(Tennessee, 1933)

The purpose of the TVA was seen by many New Deal planners as an effort to 'rescue' the farmers and hill people of the South from archaic practices that existed because of lack of electricity. Hine's role was to document this lifestyle.

PLATE 15

Lewis Hine
Women and Children on the Porch
(Tennessee, 1933)

A now-forgotten fact of rural life in the 1930s was that in much of the South, electricity was simply unavailable to those living outside towns or cities.

To address this shortcoming, as well as to create jobs, the New Deal embarked on great electrification projects. This led to the creation of such agencies as the Tennessee Valley Authority (TVA).

Just as the FSA was organized to serve the needs of farmers while employing photographers, both the TVA and Rural Electrification Administration (REA) provided aid to farmers (in the form of inexpensive electricity) and employed photographers to document their activities.

PLATE 16

George Alexander Grant
Tourists
(White Sands National Monument, New Mexico, 1934)

George Alexander Grant watched the nation slip slowly into the Depression. His work showed a different side of the times.

While Dorothea Lange and Arthur Rothstein followed the streams of Americans on the move because they were literally displaced, others still travelled on a whim, although less often. This cool day, 6 November 1934, was quiet. Few people were visiting the parks in 1934.

PLATE 17

George Alexander Grant
Waitresses in Swiss Costumes,
Many Glacier Lodge
(Glacier National Park,
Montana, 1933)

As photographed by Grant the day after an Independence Day celebration, this group of young women were typical of those who travelled from the big cities of the Midwest—especially Minneapolis and St Paul—to work as waitresses in Glacier National Park. Despite the depths of the Depression, or because of it, America thrived on escapism, hence the Swiss costumes. The women were lucky to have these jobs.

Plate 18

George Alexander Grant
Train Station
(Glacier National Park,
Montana, 1934)

The *Empire Builder* pulls into Glacier Park Station (now East Glacier) on 12 June 1934. Because the company had invested heavily in the development of rustic resort lodges in Glacier National Park, the Great Northern Railway maintained passenger service to the park from Chicago, Minneapolis and St Paul during the depths of the Depression. Business, while hardly at the levels seen in the 1920s, remained steady.

Plate 19

Plate 20

George Alexander Grant
Navajo Group
(Canyon de Chelly National
Monument, Arizona, 1934)

George Alexander Grant
Grandmother and Granddaughter
(Canyon de Chelly National
Monument, Arizona, 1934)

Native Americans were isolated from the mainstream, but not from the friendly hand of the New Deal. Grant documented this group on the floor of Canyon de Chelly on 21 September 1934 as they gathered for a presentation from personnel of the Soil Conservation Service.

In some ways, Native Americans were isolated from the Great Depression. Conditions had been as bad *before* the 1930s. While most Americans enjoyed a steady increase in their standard of living, culminating in the 1920s, Native Americans existed in a netherworld of reservation life where they never really experienced the 'roar' of the 'roaring twenties.'

This scene, in the etherial quiet of Canyon de Chelly appears exactly the same as when this grandmother sat here with her own grandmother.

PLATE 21

Lewis Hine
Out of Work Men at the Docks
During the Depression
(New York City, New York, 1934)

While drought was a factor in deepening
the Depression in the Midwest, the virtual lack of international commerce impacted the job prospects of laborers at
major ports on both coasts. In 1934,
Lewis Hine found the same drawn faces
in New York City that he had encoun-
tered in the hills of Tennessee a year
before.

PLATE 22

Lewis Hine
New York City at Night
(New York City, New York, circa 1935)

In contrast with the Resettlement Administration and Farm Security Administration views of rural farm country was
another aspect of American life at the
crossroads of the 1930s. The enormous
construction projects that were undertaken included many of New York's towering skyscrapers.

　　Among the most important images
are Hine's photographs of the Manhattan skyline, which continued to grow
despite the Depression.

PLATE 23

Edward Mancuso
*Students Marching in Support of the
Longshoremen's Strike*
(San Francisco, California, 1934)

Edward Mancuso was one of Dorothea
Lange's contemporaries in San Francisco. While Lange worked as a commercial portrait photographer before the
Depression, Mancuso cut his teeth as a
news photographer with one of the city's
now long defunct daily papers. This
photograph was taken on 22 May as the
Longshoremen's Strike was gaining mo-
mentum, as well as support from the
general public.

PLATE 25

Edward Mancuso
*A Police Face-off With Demonstrators
on the Waterfront*
(San Francisco, California, 1934)

The Depression era was filled with inci-
dents of labor and general unrest. Mancuso documented the evolution of the
Longshoremen's Strike into the notorious General Strike that paralyzed San
Francisco in July 1934. This showdown,
which occurred on 3 July, was one of the
flash points.

PLATE 24

Edward Mancuso
Demonstrator Killed By Police
(San Francisco, California, 1934)

The General Strike in San Francisco
reached its nadir on 6 July, when the
police panicked and shot a man in the
heart of the city's business district.

PLATE 26

Walker Evans
Graveyard, Houses and Steel Mill
(Bethlehem, Pennsylvania,
November, 1935)

Stark and stunning, this image of Bethlehem, Pennsylvania summarized the proximity of life, work and death to families living in the steel country of America's industrial heartland. In 1938, this image was to appear in Archibald MacLeish's book *Land of the Free*, with the caption 'We wonder whether the great American dream was the singing of locusts out of the grass to the west and the west is behind us now: The west wind's away from us.'

Deeply analyzed by important curators and art historians over the years as an icon of urban American life at the crossroads, it remains as one of Walker Evans' most important photographs.

PLATE 27

George Alexander Grant
Mount Rushmore
(Mount Rushmore National Memorial,
South Dakota, circa 1936)

Great public works projects were a hallmark of the Depression era. Some involved roads and dams, while others were merely eccentric. The great stone heads at South Dakota's Mount Rushmore were in the latter category, although they were seen at the time as inspiring 'pride in country.'

In 1938, Congress appropriated the incredible sum of $836,000 for the project. Thankfully, most of the money went to pay the hundreds of workmen who toiled on the granite mountain. Sculptor Gutzon Borglum began work on the memorial in the heady days of 1927, but most of it was carved during the Great Depression. The first head completed, that of George Washington, was finished in 1936, and the whole project was wrapped up in October 1941, only two months before the United States entered World War II.

PLATE 28

Kenneth F Space
*Leslie Bolling, Wood Whittler
at Work*
(circa 1936)

Kenneth Space travelled through the
South in 1936 and 1937, photographing
the artistic life in various black communities for the Harmon Foundation. The
Harmon Foundation and the Commission on the Church and Race Relations
of the Federal Council of Churches
sponsored a number of exhibitions of
African-American art. Their goal was to
acquaint the public with the artistic and
creative abilities of African-Americans.

PLATE 29

Kenneth F Space
Howard University Art Class
(Washington, DC, circa 1936)

While Kenneth Space travelled exten-
sively in the South during 1936 and 1937
working with black communities for the
Harmon Foundation, he also worked in
the nation's capital, photographing subjects such as this class at Howard University, typical of the show pieces for agencies like the Federal Council of
Churches. His work clearly demonstrated the essential role of the New Deal
in the improvement of life for African-
American people.

PLATE 30

Carl Mydans
Man at Work in His Field
(Iowa, 1936)

The most important of Carl Mydans'
photographs during the Resettlement
Administration era, and later with the
Farm Security Administration, resulted
from field work done in the Plains states
and the South.

PLATE 31

Carl Mydans
Checking Soil Samples
(North Carolina, 1936)

Although the corn is high, disappoint-
ment creases the farmer's face as he fin-
gers the samples. Such a moving portrait
gives us a clue to the success that was in
store for Mydans a few years later when
he became one of *Life* magazine's most
important photographers.

PLATE 32

PLATE 33

Carl Mydans
Feeding the Chickens
(Missouri, 1936)

Carl Mydans
Discussing the Crop
(Arkansas, 1936)

This remarkably well-kept Missouri farm was part of Mydans' efforts to document successful farms. Roy Stryker wanted such images to show that the FSA was actually helping people survive and prosper during the Depression.

Images that showed hardship were useful in attracting attention to the cause and for securing appropriations from Congress, but the agency also had to show the results of money well spent.

Although Arkansas was severely affected by the drought that destroyed the agricultural economy of Oklahoma, some crops survived.

PLATE 34

Edward Wall Norton
*The Future and the
Shadow of the Past*
(Colorado, 1936)

Edward Wall Norton's work is indicative that there were, in fact, some truly important images recorded during the Depression by photographers working for state agencies. He specialized in cross-generational studies, and his photographs, such as these, considered among his best, attracted a good deal of attention, especially when they were exhibited in the late 1940s.

PLATE 35

Edward Wall Norton
Mother and Child
(Colorado, 1936)

Light from an open window draws the viewer's eye to the center of attention. The mother, while not immediately apparent, forms the sturdy, yet loving, backdrop for this important photograph. While he was studying photography in New York, Norton spent a great deal of his personal time with the Renaissance masterworks in the Metropolitan Museum. This influence is obvious in his Depression-era 'Madonna and Child.'

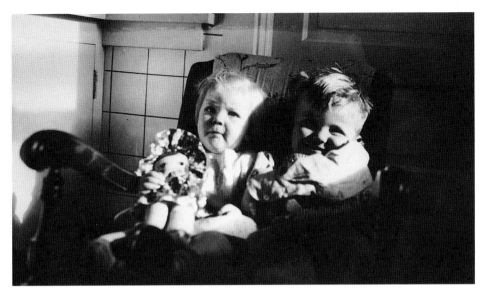

PLATE 36

PLATE 37

Edward Wall Norton
The Innocents
(Colorado, 1936)

Edward Wall Norton
The Hope of Our Future
(Colorado, 1936)

Norton's practiced eye was clearly a window on true artistic genius, as is seen in this chiaroscuro study of two children, born into the Depression, yet facing the future with a naive hope that all would be well.

PLATE 38

Arthur Rothstein
Plowing
(South Dakota, 1936)

Arthur Rothstein's Great Plains land-scapes are among the most important and most moving of any landscapes in the FSA portfolio. The image of two plow horses on paths that cross is a perfect allegory of the notion of America at the crossroads.

PLATE 39

Arthur Rothstein
Plowing
(Nebraska, 1936)

By shooting from a very low level that places the subjects near, yet beyond the horizon, Rothstein demonstrates his genius for evoking a mood that is filled with symbolism. He places the viewer in such proximity to the land that one can almost touch it.

PLATE 40

Arthur Rothstein
The Old Homestead
(Nebraska, 1936)

Dating from the Homestead era of the 1890s, Rothstein masterfully renders the sadness of a dream valiantly pursued, and grimly abandoned in the onslaught of the drought. The dreamers who once dreamed their dreams upon this homestead went west as Dust Bowl refugees and were perhaps later photographed by Rothstein himself in the migrant camps of California.

Plate 41

Arthur Rothstein
The Modern Farm
(Nebraska, 1936)

Fields plowed and planted await the promise of rain from the gathering cumulus. Rothstein's genius for landscape photography renders the symbolism of hope.

Plate 42

Benjamin W Smith
Crews at Work on the
Golden Gate Bridge
(San Francisco, California, 1936)

Born in Canada and raised in New York City, Benjamin W Smith came west to work as an engineer on the bridge project. His photographs, mostly taken in 1936, are among the most illustrative that exist. Amazingly, they came to light only following his death in 1992.

Plate 43

Benjamin W Smith
Steel Men at Work on the
Golden Gate Bridge
(San Francisco, California, 1936)

The Depression era witnessed the development of enormous construction projects that were out of scale with many that preceded them. Made possible by the availability of inexpensive skilled labor, these projects included New York's towering skyscrapers and San Francisco's huge bridges.

PLATE 44

**Rural Electrification
Administration Photo**
Sawing Wood
(circa 1937)

Just as the FSA was organized to serve the needs of rural people while employing photographers, the REA provided aid to these people in the form of inexpensive electricity, and also employed photographers to document their activities.

PLATE 45

**Rural Electrification
Administration Photo**
Carrying Water to the House
(circa 1936)

Because homes in much of the South and Mountain West, as well as elsewhere, had no electricity, the New Deal embarked on great electrification projects. These included the creation of such agencies as the Rural Electrification Administration (REA).

PLATE 46

**Rural Electrification
Administration Photo**
Churning Butter
(circa 1937)

Because of their lack of electricity, people lived a primitive, almost nineteenth century, existence.

PLATE 8

Dorothea Lange
A California Migrant, Eighteen-Year-Old Mother from Oklahoma
(Imperial Valley, California, 1937)

In March 1936, Dorothea Lange visited and documented the migrant camp near Nipomo, in California's San Luis Obispo County. Taken at Nipomo, Lange's photographs of Florence Thompson and her children were recognized classics.

In 1937, Lange returned to California's agricultural heartland. She found that little had changed. Florence Thompson was gone, but this eighteen-year-old mother from Oklahoma, whom Lange found near Holtville, had taken her place.

PLATE 48

Dorothea Lange
A Migrant Agricultural Worker
(Holtville, Imperial Valley,
California, 1937)

In February 1937, when Dorothea
Lange went into the Imperial Valley, she
had been assigned by Roy Stryker to
specifically find subjects whose images
the Resettlement Administration could
get published in the major national
magazines.

As Stryker put it, *Life* magazine was
interested in 'new migrant stuff,' which
had not, as opposed to the photographs
taken in 1936, already been widely
published.

PLATE 49

Dorothea Lange
*Migratory Mexican Field
Worker's Home*
(Imperial Valley, California, 1937)

During her February 1937 Holtville sessions, Lange photographed the camps of
migrant workers from Mexico, as well as
those from Arkansas and Oklahoma.
This man and child lived in a tiny make-
shift home at the edge of a pea field
which Lange found stiff with frost the
morning that she arrived.

Plate 50

Dorothea Lange
*Drought Refugees Waiting for
Relief Checks*
(Calipatria, Imperial Valley,
California, 1937)

In contrast to many of the migrant
workers that Lange photographed in the
Imperial Valley in 1937, this group of
men lounging on their Pontiac seem
well-fed and well-dressed.

Plate 51

Dorothea Lange
Former Tenant Farmers on Relief
(Imperial Valley, California, 1937)

Lange certainly captured the Depression's mood of despair on these faces.
Ironically, the Resettlement Administration was unable to interest the magazine
editors in most of Lange's 1937 'migrant
stuff,' as they called it. Today these images are icons.

PLATE 52

PLATE 53

Dorothea Lange
Migratory Workers
(Imperial Valley, California, 1937)

George Alexander Grant
Yakima Princess
(Pendleton, Oregon, 1937)

Lange met these migratory workers from Oklahoma as they were bathing and washing in a desert hot spring in the Imperial Valley.

On a visit to Pendleton, Oregon on 18 September 1937, George Alexander Grant created this superficially jovial, yet deeply disturbing, portrait of Nina Meninick, a Native American Princess of the Yakima tribe, as she conversed with William F Hoskins of Salem, Oregon. Among the dark undercurrents flowing through the piece are sexism and the degrading image of America's native people that was held by many white Americans, especially in the West.

PLATE 54

Edward Mancuso
On Strike Against the WPA
(San Francisco, California, 1937)

One of the bitter ironies of the Depression is seen in this image of workers that were laid off by one of the federal relief agencies set up to help the unemployed. Demonstrators are seen here blocking the entrance to a Works Progress Administration (WPA) recreation project in San Francisco.

PLATE 55

Edward Mancuso
On Strike Against the WPA
(San Francisco, California, 1937)

Even the federal relief agencies were not immune to labor unrest. In this 22 July image, laid-off employees engage in a sit-in at the WPA office in San Francisco. Edward Mancuso was one of Dorothea Lange's contemporaries, working as a news photographer for a daily newspaper in San Francisco.

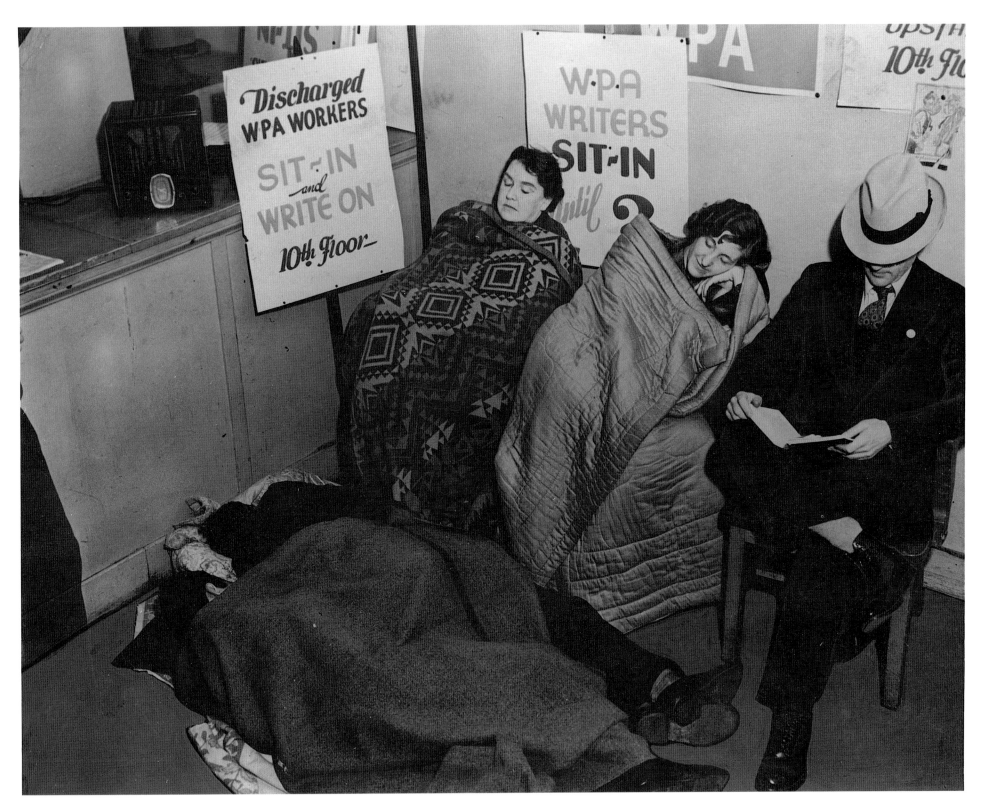

Plate 56

Arthur Rothstein
At the End of the School Day
(Gee's Bend, Alabama, 1937)

One of the stated goals of the Resettlement Administration was to focus attention on the most neglected and run-down corners of the United States. In February 1937, Roy Stryker, head of the photographic section of the RA, heard of an African-American settlement in Alabama known as Gee's Bend that was especially dilapidated and, in his words, 'primitive.'

He contacted Arthur Rothstein, who was then on assignment in Alabama, and reassigned him to Gee's Bend to take photographs for the RA's administrator to use in a presentation to Congress.

Plate 57

Arthur Rothstein
*Adell Pettway (?) on the
Pettway Plantation*
(Gee's Bend, Alabama, 1937)

As Rothstein discovered, the centerpiece of Gee's Bend was the former Pettway Plantation, on which the African-Americans, most of whose names were also Pettway, worked as sharecroppers. Rothstein's original captions for the pictures were incomplete, or have become garbled, so the identity of many of the people he photographed is uncertain. This girl is probably Adell Pettway.

PLATE 58

Arthur Rothstein
Houston or Erick Kennedy Plowing
(Gee's Bend, Alabama, 1937)

In this image it hardly matters that Rothstein didn't note which of the Kennedys was pictured. Both the impact and the broader purpose of the photograph are larger and more important than the subject.

PLATE 59

Arthur Rothstein
Artelia Bendolph
(Gee's Bend, Alabama, 1937)

Rothstein has been criticized for posing his subjects rather than photographing them as they came and went on their own. His genius, however, lay in his ability to compose a scene that was 'more real than real,' and which told the story in a fuller and more well-rounded way. In this case, his juxtaposition of images is nothing short of brilliant.

PLATE 60

PLATE 61

Arthur Rothstein
Annie Pettway Bendolph
(Gee's Bend, Alabama, 1937)

Walker Evans
People on East Sixty-first Street
(New York City, New York, 1938)

Roy Stryker needed 'primitive' imagery for the Resettlement Administration's administrator to use in a presentation to Congress and Rothstein certainly delivered a portrait of Gee's Bend that satisfied the requirement. Indeed, a great deal of media attention was devoted to Gee's Bend periodically in the 1940s and 1960s.

Walker Evans is certainly among the upper tier of great photographers of the twentieth century urban landscape and lifestyle. Although he worked in the South and produced an eloquent study of sharecroppers in Alabama for *Fortune* magazine, much of his best work was done in urban settings.

On 23 August 1938, he photographed this woman and her children on East Sixty-first Street, probably between First and Second Avenues, in New York City.

PLATE 62

Walker Evans
Children on East Sixty-first Street
(New York City, New York, 1938)

In considering the work of Evans, one is constantly reminded of his genius for interpreting the twentieth century urban landscape, which included character studies that revealed the full depth of human experience.

PLATE 63

Walker Evans
Children on East Sixty-first Street
(New York City, New York, 1938)

PLATE 64

Walker Evans
Apartment Buildings
(New York City, New York, 1938)

Evans' historic profile of New York City, photographed on 23 August 1938, included these apartment buildings at 315 and 317 East Sixty-first Street. This excellent work was produced for the FSA while Evans was waiting for his Guggenheim Fellowship.

PLATE 65

Walker Evans
Tenant on East Sixty-first Street
(New York City, New York, 1938)

The urban portraits that Evans produced during his 23 August 1938 New York City session are the dramatic complement to the best rural portraiture that Dorothea Lange produced during her California sessions of years earlier.

PLATE 66

John Vachon
At the Armistice Day Parade
(Omaha, Nebraska, 1938)

John Vachon, who was born and raised in Minnesota, came to Washington, DC to attend college. He joined the FSA as a messenger, with no thought of becoming a photographer. However, with the technical assistance of Ben Shahn and Walker Evans, he became a photographer in 1937.

His first FSA photographic assignment took him to Nebraska in November 1938. This moving portrait was taken on 11 November as the people of Omaha celebrated the twentieth anniversary of the end of World War I.

PLATE 67

John Vachon
Cars and Parking Meters
(Omaha, Nebraska, 1938)

Walker Evans' genius for turning the urban landscape into a sublime artistic expression clearly influenced much of Vachon's work in Omaha.

PLATE 68

John Vachon
*Houses Near the Nebraska Power
Company Plant*
(Omaha, Nebraska, 1938)

In a 1938 article for *Harper's* magazine, George Leighton had described Omaha as a city whose economy was dominated by its big outsider-owned power company, railroad barons and big meat packing companies, where reformers and progressives were shunned and strikes were put down violently.

As a New Deal progressive himself, FSA photographic chief Roy Stryker was interested in this and cited Leighton's article as the catalyst for sending Vachon to Omaha.

PLATE 69

John Vachon
In the Italian District
(Omaha, Nebraska, 1938)

As John Vachon recalled later, he spent a 'cold November week' in Omaha, where he 'realized that I had developed my own style with a camera.' Strongly influenced by George Leighton's indictment of Omaha's corruption, Vachon sought images that could be used to illustrate it when it appeared in book form.

This view of Italian-American homes along an electric streetcar track is dominated by the pseudo-benevolent presence of what Leighton decried as the outsider-owned power company.

PLATE 70

John Vachon
*Unemployed Men Who Ride the
Freight Trains*
(Omaha, Nebraska, November 1938)

As he spent his 'cold November week' in
Omaha, Vachon met this forlorn pair of
unemployed men who told him that
they spent their days riding freight trains
from Omaha to Kansas City and St
Louis and back.

PLATE 71

Edward Mancuso (?)
The Marvin Clark Family
(Half Moon Bay, California, 1938)

The moving images of migrant workers
that were taken by Dorothea Lange in
the California agricultural heartland in
1936 and 1937 inspired many other photographers. This photo, which may have
been taken by one of Lange's contemporaries, or even by Lange herself, shows
Marvin Clark and his family at Half
Moon Bay on 25 July as they sought
work in the coastal artichoke and
brussels sprout fields. Mrs Clark holds a
baby that was born a few weeks earlier in
Salinas.

PLATE 72

Marion Post Wolcott
Employment Agency
(Miami, Florida, 1939)

This moving image of life in South Florida is a bitter portrait of an unemployed African-American woman applying for work through an employment agency where whites were specified for most jobs.

PLATE 73

Ben Shahn
Sharecropper at Home on Sunday
(Pulaski County, Arkansas, 1935)

Two views of the South, the rural and the resort. The two worlds were so close, yet so far, but the woman in Wolcott's image probably had roots in the reality of Shahn's sharecropper.

In this portrait, one of Shahn's most moving, he is able to take us into the very heart and soul of his subject, a man whose people were desperate for survival and could hardly imagine life at a Florida resort.

PLATE 74

Marion Post Wolcott
Bar in a Private Home
(Miami, Florida, 1939)

A New Jersey-born professional photographer, Marion Post (she married Lee Wolcott in 1941) had travelled in Europe for several years before joining the FSA in 1938. While Dorothea Lange and Walker Evans produced their images of the underclass, Marion Post penetrated the comfortable, yet detached, world of the well-to-do.

PLATE 75

Marion Post Wolcott
A Meal on the Sidewalk at the Beach
(Hialeah Park, Florida, 1939)

Marion Post's images of the high life in Hialeah Park, photographed from a high angle, reveal a comfortably casual lifestyle that existed independently of the misery of the Depression and serve to remind us of the other side of life in America at the crossroads.

PLATE 76

Marion Post Wolcott
At the Beach
(Miami Beach, Florida, 1939)

Because of her long hair, brightly colored scarves and flowered dresses, FSA photographic section chief Roy Stryker felt Marion Post would be unable to move among the people whom she would photograph. In Miami Beach, this perhaps allowed her to fit in with the people who generally had a strong opposition to the New Deal and all it represented.

PLATE 77

Marion Post Wolcott
At the Beach
(Miami Beach, Florida, 1939)

Marion Post found that the wealthy who wintered in South Florida were generally suspicious of being photographed, so most of her photographs of such subjects were candid views taken at a distance.

PLATE 78

Dorothea Lange
Farm Buildings
(South Dakota, circa 1939)

The farms photographed by Lange in South Dakota were an especially poignant image, given that these were the homes of the class of people whom she had photographed in the migrant camps of California over the preceding half decade.

PLATE 79

Dorothea Lange
Buried in the Drifts
(South Dakota, circa 1939)

Dorothea Lange had to have felt a pang of sadness, seeing here the cast off dream abandoned in the face of the Dust Bowl, and knowing that the refugees had perhaps been photographed by her in the migrant camps of California.

PLATE 80

George Alexander Grant
*The Cooke City Entrance to
Yellowstone National Park*
(Cooke City, Montana, 1939)

The warm, dry days of August found
Grant driving east on US Highway 212
from Cooke City, Montana on the road
that would ultimately take him into the
canyons of the Yellowstone River, but en
route he captured an urban landscape so
distant from those observed by Walker
Evans, but at the same time so much
alike, in that they shared the dark cloud
of the Depression.

PLATE 81

George Alexander Grant
*The Cooke City Entrance to
Yellowstone National Park*
(Cooke City, Montana, 1939)

George Alexander Grant's job with the
National Park Service was to record scenic beauty, but as he travelled to the
parks, he occasionally took photographs
of the tiny towns and villages that had
sprung up around the entrances to the
parks.

Just as the Depression took its toll on
the small businesses in large cities, so too
were small merchants in tiny crossroads
forced to face the reality of declining
activity. Cooke City, Montana was such
a crossroads.

PLATE 82

Dorothea Lange
Salvation Army Marching
(San Francisco, California, 1939)

The Salvation Army was one of the many private relief agencies that were active during the Depression. In his seminal view of the era, *Grapes of Wrath*, John Steinbeck was critical of the Salvation Army, but Dorothea Lange chose it as a subject.

PLATE 83

Dorothea Lange
*Returning from the
Open-Air Meeting*
(San Francisco, California, 1939)

In this image of Salvation Army personnel returning from an open-air meeting, Lange brilliantly directs our point of view through a hotel lobby picture window.

PLATE 84

Dorothea Lange
Salvation Army Girls' Sunday School Class at the Open-Air Meeting on Minna Street
(San Francisco, California, 1939)

Lange travelled from her home in Berkeley to record this Salvation Army girls' Sunday school class at an open-air meeting on Minna Street in San Francisco.

PLATE 85

Edward Mancuso
The Federal Theater Project Goes Dark
(San Francisco, California, 1939)

Just as Edward Mancuso had recorded the irony of a strike against the Works Progress Administration in 1937, he documented the closing of the Federal Theater Project presentation of *Two A Day*, which had been playing at the Alcazar Theater in San Francisco. The New Deal had created projects to make work for writers, photographers and actors, but it could, and did, eliminate those jobs.

PLATE 86

**Rural Electrification
Administration Photo**
Airport Beacon at Twilight
(Rush County, Kansas, circa 1940)

PLATE 87

**Rural Electrification
Administration Photo**
Airport Beacon By Night
(Rush County, Kansas, circa 1940)

The Rural Electrification Administration was the perfect example of a New Deal agency that rolled up its sleeves and brought progress to the people, while providing jobs for those left idle by the Depression.

PLATE 88

**Rural Electrification
Administration Photo**
REA Co-op
(Rush County, Kansas, circa 1940)

Many federal relief agencies had been organized to serve the needs of rural people, just as the REA provided inexpensive electricity. At the same time, these agencies also employed photographers to document their activities for both public relations purposes and to aid in obtaining appropriations from Congress.

PLATE 89

**Rural Electrification
Administration Photo**
Adjusting the Radio
(circa 1940)

The availability of electricity, made possible by such agencies as the Rural Electrification Administration and Tennessee Valley Authority, opened up a new world to people who'd lived without it. In the case of radio, it was literally a new world.

PLATE 90

**Rural Electrification
Administration Photo**
Darning Socks
(circa 1940)

Just as the REA employed photographers to document the life of people who had no electricity, they employed photographers to document the life of the people after electricity was made available to them.

Plate 91

Marion Post Wolcott
Post Office During Blizzard
(Aspen, Colorado, 1941)

Just as she developed a distinctive personal style, Marion Post had a keen photographic style. Remembered for her vision and sensitivity, she stunned her colleagues and deprived the world of great creative promise by giving up documentary photography after her 1941 marriage to Lee Wolcott.

Plate 92

Edward Wall Norton
Gaming Machines
(Montana, 1940)

While Edward Wall Norton is best remembered for his thoughtful and important character studies, especially of children, his portfolio also included documentary photography. By 1940, the mood of the nation had improved, and there was thought of recreation. Norton took this photograph on a field trip to Montana during the summer of 1940.

Plate 93

Edward Wall Norton
Sunday Evening
(Colorado, 1940)

Norton's masterful ability to penetrate beneath the surface in his portraits is evident in this photograph taken at a family's Sunday dinner. Light and shadow play a subtle role, and it is clear that Norton is in command of the scene.

PLATE 94

George Alexander Grant
Thunderbird Ranch
(Near Canyon de Chelly National
Monument, Arizona, 1940)

Grant's contribution to the portfolio of images depicting America at the crossroads was in large measure to show us things that changed at a vastly slower pace. In urban areas, it was possible for a 'crash' to cause sudden, violent change. At the Thunderbird Ranch in Arizona,

which Grant visited on 17 June 1940, many things, indeed life itself, had probably changed little since 1890.

Grant's *Thunderbird Ranch* becomes an architectural study, comparing the old adobe structure in the lower right, which dates from the native-influences

Hispanic period, to the pioneer-style utilitarian log buildings with their roots in the nineteenth or even eighteenth century, and finally the American-style wood frame buildings at the center of the complex, which, in Arizona, probably date from about 1890.

PLATE 95

Dorothea Lange
Yaquii Indian 'Jacal'
(Pinal County, Arizona, 1940)

Dorothea Lange crossed George Alexander Grant's path in 1940, bringing her camera and brilliant insight into the human condition into Arizona's Pinal County. As in California and the South, she studied the agricultural communities, and in this case, Cortaro Farms, where Native Americans lived upon and worked the land of their ancestors with the generous assistance of New Deal programs. By photographing this 'jacal,' or dwelling, without people, Dorothea Lange has created a stunning allegory for the timelessness of life and the history of civilization in the American Southwest. The buildings themselves are constructed in the traditional manner, using mud, cactus ribs and mesquite timbers.

PLATE 96

Dorothea Lange
*Letting Down the Sack From
The Scales*
(Pinal County, Arizona, 1940)

This image is one of the most important of Dorothea Lange's photographs at Cortaro Farms. She has masterfully demonstrated the man's deft toss of the rope by using a slow shutter speed. After the passage of many decades, the rope is still in motion as it was on this November afternoon in 1940.

PLATE 97

Dorothea Lange
Mexican Irrigator
(Pinal County, Arizona, 1940)

Following the path of the Spanish Conquistadors, this man came from Mexico 12 years ago and worked year-round on this large farm. Like many, first generation immigrants in the 40s and even today, he worked as a laborer, doing the work that many US citizens refuse to dirty their hands with. Yet the migrant workers, legal and illegal, remain the scapegoat of politicians and racism, blamed for economic problems that existed long before they arrived in this country.

   In this timeless photograph, Lange has captured the ultimate dignity of a man who works with his hands, proud of both his past and his future, knowing that the nation depends on people like himself.

PLATE 98

Jack Delano
Polish Tobacco Farmers
(Connecticut, 1940)

Mr and Mrs Andrew Lyman smiled happily for Jack Delano in 1940, but their tobacco farm near Windsor Locks had been a recipient of FSA aid for some time.

Delano, a former student of painting at the Pennsylvania Academy of Fine Arts, came to the FSA as a photographer in 1940. Roy Stryker sent him on numerous assignments, including Puerto Rico, where he documented the economic development work being undertaken under the direction of Rexford Tugwell, an old friend of Stryker's and one of the men who influenced the decision to set up a photographic section within the Resettlement Administration.

PLATE 99

Arthur Rothstein
Vegetable Garden
(Visalia, California, 1940)

The migrant worker camp at Visalia originated in 1934 as a temporary relief center constructed by California's state government. In 1935, it was taken over by the federal government's Resettlement Administration.

By 1937, when it came under the jurisdiction of the FSA, the Visalia migrant camp had grown into a huge, permanent 'city,' with a population swollen by a tide of new refugees from Oklahoma and Arkansas.

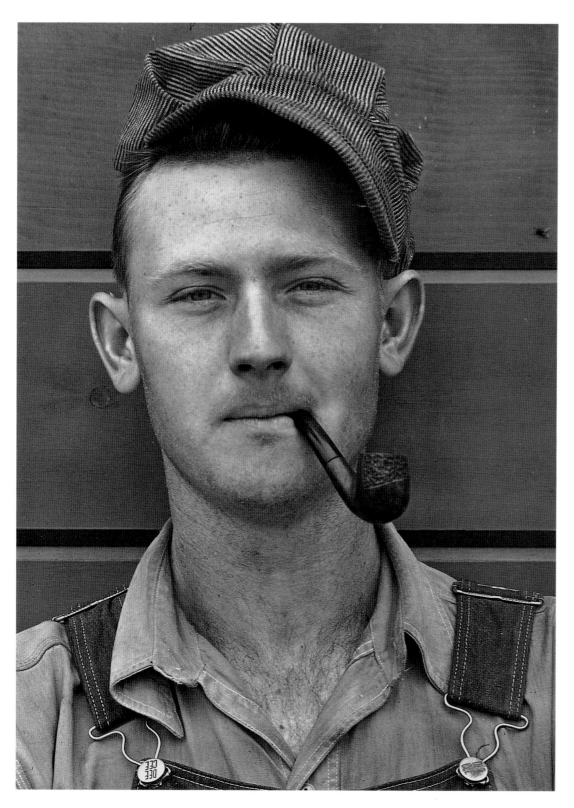

Plate 100

Arthur Rothstein
Camp Resident
(Visalia, California, 1940)

FSA photographic section chief Roy Stryker was anxious to document the huge Visalia migrant workers' camp and picked Arthur Rothstein because of his magnificent and well-received work at Gee's Bend, Alabama three years earlier.

PLATE 101

Arthur Rothstein
Camp Resident
(Visalia, California, 1940)

Compared to what they had left behind
in Oklahoma, migrant workers found
the Visalia migrant camp to be a refuge, a
port in the storm of socioeconomic up-
heaval that had gripped the nation.

PLATE 102

Arthur Rothstein
Camp Resident
(Visalia, California, 1940)

Arthur Rothstein's masterful Visalia portrait series had provided some of the most important views of the face of humanity during the Great Depression.

PLATE 103

Arthur Rothstein
Camp Resident
(Visalia, California, 1940)

Rothstein, who had documented the important site at Gee's Bend, Alabama, as well as having produced many memorable midwestern landscape series, was sent to California in 1940. There was continuing interest in photographs of California migrant camps on the part of the national publications to whom the FSA supplied material.

PLATE 104

Arthur Rothstein
Fixing a Truck
(Visalia, California, 1940)

In this image, the vehicle that carried this family from Arkansas becomes an allegory for the end of the rainbow. Rothstein's use of powerful cloud formations as a backdrop was a major element of his photographic style.

PLATE 105

Arthur Rothstein
In the Recreation Hall
(Visalia, California, 1940)

Life in the communally organized Visalia migrant camp was a far cry from the miserable camps that had existed in the state's agricultural valleys in the mid-1930s. However, many local residents disliked the camp, which they perceived as being tainted with communism as a political doctrine.

PLATE 106

Arthur Rothstein
Custer State Park Scene
(Custer State Park, South Dakota, 1936)

In May 1936, during Rothstein's survey of the farms of the upper Midwest, he went into the Black Hills country. Here we find the ancestral land of the Dakota people being contemplated by non-Natives. Rothstein's image is juxtaposed to Grant's image of a descendant of America's indigenous people.

PLATE 107

George Alexander Grant
Jimmy Hudson
(Priest Rapids, Washington, 1941)

There was optimism in the air about the end of the Depression on 26 June 1941, when George Alexander Grant photographed this young Native American along the Columbia River at Priest Rapids, Washington. Note the denim jeans and Lucky Strike package that are emblematic of the way the mainstream culture had impacted a traditional lifestyle which, as late as the 1940s, still included pinto ponies and long braids.

Nearby was the new Priest Rapids Dam, one of the series of hydroelectric projects that would not have existed if not for the Depression, and which brought Native Americans further into the mainstream.

PLATE 108

Russell Lee
The Guesser on the Midway
(Vale, Oregon, 1941)

How will he do? How will he do it? There is something in the spirit that loves a mystery.

The history of American county fairs, indeed the history of rural festivals since the dawn of civilization, includes the sleight of hand artist, the snake charmer, the patent medicine man and charming nine-year-old who deftly separates you from your pocket change as he amuses you.

PLATE 109

Russell Lee
*Pledge of Allegiance at the
Baseball Field*
(Vale, Oregon, 1941)

Few images of American life can be more moving than the pledge of allegiance at the baseball field on Independence Day, especially *this*, the Independence Day that rests at the pivotal moment between the Depression and the United States' entry into World War II. America soon will have passed the crossroads, and set a course for the future, a very different future.

PLATE 110

Russell Lee
Outside the Red Robin Cafe
(Vale, Oregon, 1941)

If the small town is the crossroads of the
American spirit, and its center is its Main
Street, then the nexus of that main street
is the cafe where everyone in town comes
and goes.

The cafe is the crossroads within the
crossroads. Lee brilliantly shows us two
points of view, looking in and looking
out.

PLATE 111

Russell Lee
Cold Drinks Inside the
Red Robin Cafe
(Vale, Oregon, 1941)

PLATE 112

Russell Lee
Family Picnic
(Vale, Oregon, 1941)

In his legendary Independence Day series, Lee takes us to the very heartland of the American spirit. He takes familiar images, transforming them from the stereotypical to the sublime.

Plate 113

Russell Lee
After Lunch
(Vale, Oregon, 1941)

PLATE 114

PLATE 115

Russell Lee
Motorcycle With Stunt Bars
(Vale, Oregon, 1941)

Russell Lee
*Independence Day, Motorcyclist
and Friends*
(Vale, Oregon, 1941)

In the Independence Day series Lee moves from a focus on Main Street as a metaphor for main streets everywhere to a view of the archetypical American vagabond for whom the highway is Main Street.

An image of America, an image of an America to come, the biker from Baker, Oregon and the local girls from Vale. Lee has captured an extraordinary scene that takes us from the desperation of the Depression years to an image of a very different sort of uprooted America that is to come a quarter century in the future.

This image clearly reminds us that the children of these people will live in an America that will face an entirely different crossroads in the middle 1960s.

122

PLATE 116

John Collier, Jr
Juan Lopez
(Trampas, New Mexico, 1943)

Though it took place a year after the Farm Security Administration's photographic section was transferred to the Office of War Information (OWI), John Collier's series of photographs of the Juan Lopez family home near Trampas, New Mexico are seen as the final series in the body of work which began under the auspices of the Resettlement Administration in 1935.

PLATE 117

John Collier, Jr
The Juan Lopez Family
(Trampas, New Mexico, 1943)

In this view, the family gathers in grandfather Juan Romero's room for a quiet moment of togetherness. Collier achieved the shadow effects with a single bare photographic bulb in the fireplace.

Photographic section chief Roy Stryker opposed Collier's idea of a New Mexico session, but ultimately he agreed, albeit reluctantly. Eventually, photos from this series became part of the *Portrait of America* series published by the OWI.

INDEX

Overleaf:

PLATE 118

John Collier, Jr
*A Bedroom in the Juan Lopez
Family Home*
(Trampas, New Mexico, 1943)

The morning sun falls across the bed in
this timeless room. Most of the furnish-
ings date from the nineteenth century,
but the portrait of Mr Lopez is from
World War I and the bed could be from
the eighteenth century.